BUCKY & DAISY'S MOODY ADVENTURES DISCOVER: EXERCISE

Written & Characters By:
Donna Fatigato

Illustrated By: Cheyenne Davis

Copyright © 2021 - All Rights Reserved

Published by Lulu Press Inc.

ISBN: 978-1733941532

THIS BOOK IS DEDICATED TO YOU!
NAME: _____
WELCOME TO HEALTHY TOWN!

Bucky and Daisy
love to play…

But their moods changed suddenly one day!

and Daisy wanted to sleep.

Their mom and dad didn't hear a peep.

Perhaps a bike ride, walk or hike

Will help them out of their snoozy state

so they don't fall asleep

in their dinner plate.

Healthy food, water and exercise go hand-in-hand

so they decided to design a plan.

To keep them healthy, strong and awake

to fuel their heart, lungs, muscles and brain.

Moving and jumping and...
eating just right

will help them to rest and sleep,
like they should at night.

Nighty night, sleep tight

and when you awake,

we will move our bodies to feel great!

Parent's Corner

Count how many times you can bounce and catch the ball in a row.

Count how many times you can throw the ball up in the air and catch it.

Draw four large squares with chalk and write a category in each square like colors, books, sports, food. Take turns with one person bouncing the ball in the first square and stating a color, then bouncing the ball in the second square stating a book, etc. until they have finished all four squares. Either go again or take turns, if playing with multiple people. This is a great exercise for the mind/body connection plus coordination!

Count how many times you can kick the ball between two objects - like a cone or plastic bottle.

Kick the ball from one object to the other and see how many times you can kick it back and forth remaining close to the objects. Change the distance of objects accordingly.

Jump rope, bike, hike, hopscotch, jumping jacks and running drills are all simple ways to keep your children moving, happy and healthy! Enjoy!

Donna Fatigato brings her characters to life to teach future generations about health, wellness and nutrition.

Donna is a proud wife, mother and nonna and enjoys mentoring, cooking and teaching mind-body practices - like Yoga and Pilates.

You can learn more at: www.Q2Fit.com

The Bucky & Daisy's Moody Adventures
Book Collection

All rights reserved.

Copyright © 2021 Donna Fatigato

ISBN: 978-1733941532

For permission requests,
please contact the author at

donna@q2fit.com

www.ingramcontent.com/pod-product-compliance
Lightning Source LLC
Chambersburg PA
CBHW041633040426
42446CB00024B/3494